D1549771

BEST OF GREECE

Consultant Editor:
Valerie Ferguson

LORENZ BOOKS

Contents

Introduction

The Greeks enjoy the simple things in life: sun, sea and fresh air. They also like to eat well, and after centuries of experimenting they have developed an exquisite cuisine that is enjoyed throughout the world. The country's location means that its cooking has benefited from both Eastern and Western influences, creating an array of uniquely delicious tastes. Popular ingredients include olive oil, fresh tomatoes and lemons.

Central to Greek cuisine is *meze,* a small portion of something delicious. This can be a creamy dip, a plate of elaborately stuffed vegetables or even just a few black olives.

In rural areas, people tend to eat what is produced locally. Tangy Avgolemono Soup makes the most of the lemon harvest while Greek Lamb Sausages with Tomato Sauce benefits from the flavour of home-grown tomatoes. Horta, a wild vegetable similar to spinach and strong in iron content, and okra are also favourites. Parts of Greece are renowned for particular products, such as olives from Kalamata, honeydew melons from Argos and grapes from Crete. Fruit, such as melons, grapes, apricots and peaches, is plentiful.

In *Best of Greece* you will find an authentic flavour of this varied cuisine.

Ingredients

A walk through a Greek market provides a wonderful introduction to local ingredients. Shop after shop is packed with aromatics and spices, and colourful displays of fruit and vegetables constantly catch the eye.

CONDIMENTS

The most widely used condiment in Greek cooking is olive oil. With its slightly peppery flavour it enhances both cooked dishes and salads. Other useful ingredients are olives, tahini (sesame seed paste), Greek honey and filo pastry, which will keep in the freezer for several months.

DAIRY PRODUCE

Greece is famous for Halloumi, Feta and Kefalotiri cheeses made from goat's and sheep's milk. Halloumi is often grilled, while Feta is used in salads. Rich, creamy Greek yogurt is used in both savoury and sweet dishes.

FISH & SEAFOOD

Many Greek recipes feature the abundant range of fish and seafood in the region such as cod, whitebait, calamari (squid) and octopus.

FRUIT

The warm climate of Greece produces many delicious seasonal fruits including lemons, oranges, grapes for the table and wine, melons and figs.

HERBS & SPICES

Herbs such as coriander, thyme, garlic, rosemary, mint, oregano, dill and parsley are used liberally for their flavour and health-giving properties.

A selection of nuts, clockwise from top left: pistachio nuts, pine nuts, hazelnuts, almonds, and walnuts.

Spices are usually used in their ground form and favourites include cinnamon, cumin, nutmeg, paprika and saffron strands which add a spicy warmth and flavour to a wide variety of dishes.

A selection of fresh herbs, clockwise from top left: dill, flat leaf parsley, mint, marjoram and coriander (centre).

POULTRY & MEAT
Greek cuisine has many famous meat dishes such as moussaka and kleftiko. Lamb is most widely used but chicken and beef are also popular.

NUTS & SEEDS
Nuts are widely used in Greek cooking and are often combined with rice. Almonds, hazelnuts, pistachios, pine nuts and sesame seeds are found in savouries and sweetmeats, such as the spicy pie, baklava.

PULSES & GRAINS
Many starters and soups include pulses, such as chick-peas in hummus and lentils in faki. Rice is also a common

ingredient for stuffing vegetables and serving with kebabs. Long grain is mainly used for savoury dishes.

VEGETABLES
No Greek meal would be complete without an array of raw and cooked vegetable dishes. Aubergines and tomatoes are perhaps the two which feature most, but there are many others which are associated with Greece. Spinach is used in many dishes, as are red peppers which can be stuffed or cooked with meat and aubergines. When grilled they acquire a smoky flavour, and are a tasty salad ingredient. Vine leaves are used to wrap an aromatic rice mixture for dolmades, while the delicate flavour of shelled and skinned broad beans are a wonderful addition to casseroles.

7

Techniques

CRUSHING SPICES

1 Crush whole spices in a coffee grinder. Keep one specifically for this purpose.

2 Alternatively, crush spices in a mortar with a pestle. This is especially good for small quantities.

CHOPPING HERBS

1 Remove any thick stalks, then use a sharp knife to chop the leaves finely on a board.

2 Alternatively, use a two-handled herb chopper, also called a mezzaluna. Rock the blade from side to side.

PREPARING GARLIC

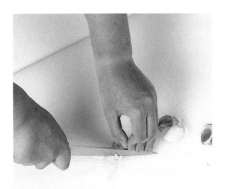

1 Break off the clove of garlic, place the flat side of a large knife on top and strike with your fist. Remove all the papery outer skin. Begin by finely chopping the clove.

2 Sprinkle over a little table salt and, using the flat side of a large knife blade, work the salt into the garlic, until the clove softens and releases its juices. Use as required.

STONING OLIVES

1 To remove the stone from an olive, put the olive in the stoner, pointed end uppermost.

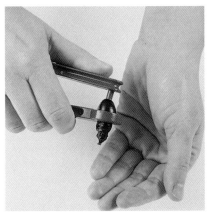

2 Squeeze the handles of the stoner together to extract the stone. Using a stoner is the easiest way to remove the stone from an olive, but you can also use a sharp knife.

Hot Halloumi with Roasted Peppers

A salty, hard cheese, halloumi is delicious served simply sliced or cubed.
It also takes on a wonderful texture when grilled or fried.

Serves 4

INGREDIENTS
6 red, green or yellow peppers
olive oil
30 ml/2 tbsp balsamic or red wine vinegar
small handful of raisins (optional)
300 g/11 oz halloumi cheese, thickly sliced
salt and freshly ground black pepper
flat leaf parsley, to garnish
Olive and Oregano Bread, to serve (optional)

1 Preheat the oven to 220°C/425°F/
Gas 7. Cut the peppers into
quarters, discard the cores and seeds,
then place cut side down on a baking
sheet. Roast for 20 minutes until the
skins start to blacken and blister.

2 Remove and cover with several layers
of kitchen paper. Set aside for 30
minutes, then peel off the skins. Slice
the flesh into a bowl. Save any roasting
juices and mix these with the peppers.

3 Pour a little olive oil over the
roasted peppers. Add the vinegar
and raisins, if using, with salt and
pepper to taste. Toss the salad lightly
and leave to cool.

4 When ready to serve, divide the
pepper salad among four plates.
Heat olive oil to a depth of about
5 mm/¼ in in a large heavy-based
frying pan. Fry the halloumi slices over
a medium-high heat for about 2–3
minutes, turning them halfway
through cooking until golden brown
on both sides.

5 Drain the fried halloumi
thoroughly on kitchen paper and
serve with the roasted pepper salad and
a parsley garnish. Offer chunks of
Olive and Oregano Bread to soak up
the juices, if you like.

COOK'S TIPS: For a crisp coating
on the halloumi, toss the slices in
plain flour before frying them. Plain
halloumi can be grilled instead of
fried. Simply preheat a grill or
ridged grilling pan, add the cheese
slices and cook until golden brown,
turning once. They are good grilled
on a barbecue, too.

Hummus

This creamy purée is delicious as part of a *meze*, or as a dip.

Serves 4–6

INGREDIENTS
150 g/5 oz/¾ cup dried chick-peas
juice of 2 lemons
2 garlic cloves, sliced
30 ml/2 tbsp olive oil
pinch of cayenne pepper
150 ml/¼ pint/⅔ cup tahini paste
salt and freshly ground black pepper
extra olive oil and cayenne pepper,
    for sprinkling
flat leaf parsley, to garnish

1 Put the chick-peas in a bowl with plenty of cold water and leave them to soak overnight.

2 Drain the chick-peas and cover with fresh water in a saucepan. Boil rapidly for 10 minutes. Reduce the heat and simmer gently for about 1 hour, until soft. Drain.

3 Process the chick-peas in a food processor to a smooth purée. Add the lemon juice, garlic, olive oil, cayenne pepper and tahini and blend until creamy, scraping the mixture down from the sides of the bowl.

4 Season with salt and pepper and transfer to a serving dish. Sprinkle with olive oil and cayenne pepper and garnish with parsley.

Taramasalata

This version is more delicious than commercially produced taramasalata.

Serves 4

INGREDIENTS
115 g/4 oz smoked mullet roe
2 garlic cloves, crushed
30 ml/2 tbsp grated onion
60 ml/4 tbsp olive oil
4 slices white bread,
  crusts removed
juice of 2 lemons
30 ml/2 tbsp water or milk
paprika, to garnish (optional)

1 Place the smoked mullet roe, garlic, onion, olive oil, bread and lemon juice in a blender or food processor and process until smooth.

2 Add the water or milk and process again for a few seconds. (This will give the taramasalata a creamier taste.)

3 Pour the taramasalata into a serving bowl, cover with clear film and chill for 1–2 hours before serving. Just before serving, sprinkle with a little paprika, if liked.

COOK'S TIP: Since the roe of grey mullet is expensive, smoked cod's roe is often used instead for this dish. It is paler than the burnt-orange colour of mullet roe, but is still very good.

Tzatziki

Serve this refreshing yogurt dip with strips of toasted pitta bread.

Serves 4

INGREDIENTS
1 mini cucumber
4 spring onions
1 garlic clove
200 ml/7 fl oz/scant 1 cup Greek-style yogurt
45 ml/3 tbsp chopped fresh mint
salt and freshly ground black pepper
fresh mint and dill sprigs, to garnish

3 Beat the yogurt until smooth, if necessary, then gently stir in the cucumber, onions, garlic and mint.

1 Trim the ends from the cucumber, but do not peel. Cut it into 5 mm/ ¼ in dice.

4 Transfer the mixture to a serving bowl and add salt and plenty of pepper to taste. Chill until ready to serve and then garnish with small mint and dill sprigs.

COOK'S TIP: Choose Greek-style yogurt for this dip – it has a higher fat content than most yogurts, which gives it a deliciously rich, creamy texture.

2 Trim the spring onions and then, with a sharp knife, chop the onions and the peeled garlic very finely.

Dolmades

These dainty vine leaf parcels are traditionally served as part of a Greek *meze* and make a popular snack.

Serves 4

INGREDIENTS
8 vine leaves
green and red pepper salad, to serve

FOR THE FILLING
15 ml/1 tbsp olive oil
115 g/4 oz/1 cup minced beef
30 ml/2 tbsp pine nuts
1 onion, chopped
15 ml/1 tbsp chopped fresh coriander
5 ml/1 tsp ground cumin
15 ml/1 tbsp tomato purée
salt and freshly ground black pepper

FOR THE TOMATO SAUCE
150 ml/¼ pint/⅔ cup passata
150 ml/¼ pint/⅔ cup beef stock
10 ml/2 tsp caster sugar

1 For the filling, heat the oil in a pan. Add the minced beef, pine nuts and onion. Cook for 5 minutes, until brown and sealed.

2 Stir in the fresh coriander, cumin and tomato purée. Cook for a further 3 minutes and season well.

3 Lay the vine leaves shiny side down on a work surface. Place some of the cooked filling in the centre of each vine leaf and fold the stalk end over the filling. Roll up the parcel towards the tip of the leaf and place in a lightly greased flameproof casserole, seam side down.

4 For the sauce, mix together the passata, stock and sugar and pour over each vine leaf. Cover and cook on a moderate heat for 3–4 minutes. Reduce the heat and cook for a further 30 minutes. Serve with green and red pepper salad.

COOK'S TIP: If vine leaves are unavailable, use lettuce or cabbage leaves dropped in boiling water until they have wilted.

Faki

Red or puy lentils can be substituted for the green ones used in this soup.

Serves 4–6

INGREDIENTS
225 g/8 oz/1 cup green lentils
75 ml/5 tbsp olive oil
3 onions, finely chopped
2 garlic cloves, thinly sliced
10 ml/2 tsp cumin seeds, crushed
1.5 ml/¼ tsp ground turmeric
600 ml/1 pint/2½ cups chicken or
   vegetable stock
salt and freshly ground black pepper
30 ml/2 tbsp roughly chopped fresh
   coriander, to garnish
warm bread, to serve

1 Put the lentils in a saucepan and cover with cold water. Boil rapidly for 10 minutes. Drain.

2 Heat 30 ml/2 tbsp of the oil in a pan and fry two of the onions with the garlic, cumin and turmeric, stirring, for 3 minutes. Add the lentils, stock and 600 ml/1 pint/2½ cups water. Bring to the boil, reduce the heat, cover and simmer gently for 30 minutes, until the lentils are soft.

3 Fry the third onion in the remaining oil until golden. Use a potato masher to lightly mash the lentils and make the soup pulpy.

4 Reheat gently and season with salt and pepper to taste. Pour into bowls. Stir the fresh coriander into the fried onion and scatter over the soup. Serve with warm bread.

Avgolemono

The name of this popular Greek soup means egg and lemon.

Serves 4–6

INGREDIENTS
1.75 litres/3 pints/7½ cups
   chicken stock
115 g/4 oz/½ cup orzo pasta
3 eggs
juice of 1 large lemon
salt and freshly ground black pepper
lemon slices, to garnish

1 Pour the stock into a large pan, and bring to the boil. Add the pasta and cook for 5 minutes.

COOK'S TIP: If orzo pasta is unavailable, any small shape may be substituted.

2 Beat the eggs until frothy, then add the lemon juice and a tablespoon of cold water. Stir in a ladleful of hot stock, then one or two more. Return to the pan, off the heat, and stir well.

3 Do not let the soup boil once the eggs have been added or it will start to curdle. Season with salt and pepper and serve at once, garnished with lemon slices.

Marides

A spicy coating on these deep-fried whitebait gives this favourite Greek dish a special crunchy bite. This also makes an excellent starter.

Serves 6

INGREDIENTS
115 g/4 oz/1 cup plain flour
2.5 ml/½ tsp paprika
2.5 ml/½ tsp ground cayenne pepper
pinch of salt
1.2 kg/2½ lb fresh or frozen
    whitebait, thawed
vegetable oil, for deep frying
lemon wedges, to garnish

1 Mix together the flour, paprika, cayenne pepper and salt in a large bowl. Use the mixture to coat the whitebait thoroughly, stirring gently with a large spoon.

2 Heat the oil in a large, heavy-based saucepan until it reaches a temperature of 190°C/375°F. Fry the whitebait in batches for 2–3 minutes, until the fish is golden and crispy.

3 Drain well on absorbent kitchen paper. Serve hot, garnished with lemon wedges.

Fish Plaki

Generally, fish is treated very simply in Greece, but this recipe is a little more involved, baking the fish with onions, tomatoes and fresh herbs.

Serves 6

INGREDIENTS
300 ml/½ pint/1¼ cups olive oil
2 onions, thinly sliced
3 large well-flavoured tomatoes,
   roughly chopped
3 garlic cloves, thinly sliced
5 ml/1 tsp sugar
5 ml/1 tsp chopped fresh dill
5 ml/1 tsp chopped fresh mint
5 ml/1 tsp chopped fresh celery leaves
15 ml/1 tbsp chopped fresh parsley
6 firm white fish steaks
juice of 1 lemon
salt and freshly ground black pepper
extra dill, mint or parsley, to garnish

1 Heat the oil in a large sauté pan or flameproof dish. Add the onions and cook until pale golden. Add the tomatoes, garlic, sugar, dill, mint, celery leaves and parsley with 300 ml/½ pint/ 1¼ cups water. Season with salt and pepper, then simmer, uncovered, for 25 minutes, until the liquid has reduced by one-third.

2 Add the fish and cook gently for 10–12 minutes, until just cooked. Remove from the heat and add the lemon juice. Cover and stand for about 20 minutes. Arrange in a dish and spoon the sauce over. Garnish with herbs and serve warm or cold.

Stuffed Calamari

This Greek delicacy is best made with large squid as they are less fiddly to stuff. If you have to make do with small squid, buy about 450 g/1 lb.

Serves 4

INGREDIENTS
4 squid tubes, each about 18 cm/7 in long
900 g/2 lb ripe tomatoes
45 ml/3 tbsp olive oil
1 large onion, chopped
5 ml/1 tsp caster sugar
120 ml/4 fl oz/½ cup dry white wine
several rosemary sprigs
toasted pine nuts and flat leaf parsley,
   to garnish

FOR THE STUFFING
30 ml/2 tbsp olive oil
1 large onion, finely chopped
2 garlic cloves, crushed
50 g/2 oz/1 cup fresh breadcrumbs
60 ml/4 tbsp chopped fresh parsley
115 g/4 oz halloumi cheese, grated
salt and freshly ground black pepper

1 To make the stuffing, heat the oil in a frying pan and fry the onion for 3 minutes. Remove the pan from the heat and add the garlic, breadcrumbs, parsley, cheese and a little salt and pepper. Stir until thoroughly blended.

2 Dry the squid tubes on kitchen paper and fill with the prepared stuffing using a teaspoon. Secure the ends of the squid tubes with wooden cocktail sticks.

3 Plunge the tomatoes into boiling water for 30 seconds, then refresh in cold water. Skin and chop roughly.

4 Heat the oil in a frying pan or sauté pan. Add the squid and fry on all sides. Remove from the pan.

5 Add the onion to the pan and fry gently for 3 minutes. Stir in the tomatoes, sugar and wine and cook rapidly until the mixture becomes thick and pulpy.

6 Return the squid to the pan with the rosemary. Cover and cook gently for 30 minutes. Slice the squid and serve on individual plates with the sauce. Scatter over the pine nuts and garnish with parsley.

VARIATION: If you would prefer a less rich filling, halve the quantity of halloumi cheese and breadcrumbs in the stuffing and add 225 g/8 oz cooked spinach.

Octopus & Red Wine Stew

Unless you are happy to clean and prepare octopus for this dish, buy one that is ready for cooking.

Serves 4

INGREDIENTS
900 g/2 lb prepared octopus
450 g/1 lb onions, sliced
2 bay leaves
450 g/1 lb ripe tomatoes
60 ml/4 tbsp olive oil
4 garlic cloves, crushed
5 ml/1 tsp caster sugar
15 ml/1 tbsp chopped fresh oregano or
  rosemary
30 ml/2 tbsp chopped fresh parsley
150 ml/¼ pint/⅔ cup red wine
30 ml/2 tbsp red wine vinegar
chopped fresh herbs, to garnish
warm bread and pine nuts, to serve

3 Drain the octopus and, using a sharp knife, cut it into bite-size pieces. Discard the head.

4 Heat the oil in a saucepan and fry the octopus, the remaining onions and the garlic for 3 minutes. Add the tomatoes, sugar, oregano or rosemary, parsley, wine and vinegar and cook, stirring, for 5 minutes until pulpy.

1 Put the octopus in a saucepan of gently simmering water with a quarter of the onions and the bay leaves. Cook gently for 1 hour.

2 Meanwhile, plunge the tomatoes into boiling water for 30 seconds, then refresh in cold water. Peel away the skins and chop roughly.

5 Cover the pan and cook over the lowest possible heat for about 1½ hours until the sauce is thickened and the octopus is tender. Garnish the stew with fresh herbs and serve with plenty of warm bread, and pine nuts to scatter over the top.

Chicken & Olives

Slow cooking infuses the chicken with the delicious flavours of the Mediterranean – garlic, onions, lemon and olives.

Serves 4

INGREDIENTS
30 ml/2 tbsp olive oil
1.5 kg/3–3½ lb chicken
1 large onion, sliced
15 ml/1 tbsp grated fresh root ginger
3 garlic cloves, crushed
5 ml/1 tsp paprika
250 ml/8 fl oz/1 cup chicken stock
2–3 saffron strands, soaked in 15 ml/1 tbsp
    boiling water
4–5 spring onions, chopped
15–20 black and green olives,
    stoned
juice of ½ lemon
salt and freshly ground black pepper

TO SERVE
cooked rice
mixed salad

1 Heat the oil in a large saucepan or flameproof casserole and sauté the chicken on both sides until golden.

2 Add the onion, ginger, garlic, paprika and seasoning and continue frying over a moderate heat, coating the chicken with the mixture.

3 Add the chicken stock and saffron and bring to the boil. Cover and simmer gently for 45 minutes, or until the chicken is well done.

4 Add the spring onions and cook for a further 15 minutes until the chicken is well cooked and the sauce is reduced to about 120 ml/ 4 fl oz/½ cup.

5 Add the black and green olives and lemon juice and cook for a further 5 minutes. Remove from the heat.

6 Place the chicken on a large deep plate and pour over the sauce. Serve with rice and a mixed salad.

Kotopitta

Serve hot or cold with a typical Greek salad made from tomatoes, cucumber, onions and feta cheese.

Serves 4

INGREDIENTS
275 g/10 oz filo pastry
30 ml/2 tbsp olive oil
75 g/3 oz/½ cup chopped
    toasted almonds
30 ml/2 tbsp milk

FOR THE FILLING
15 ml/1 tbsp olive oil
1 medium onion, finely chopped
1 garlic clove, crushed
450 g/1 lb boned and cooked chicken
50 g/2 oz feta cheese, crumbled
2 eggs, beaten
15 ml/1 tbsp chopped fresh parsley
15 ml/1 tbsp chopped
    fresh coriander
15 ml/1 tbsp chopped fresh mint
salt and freshly ground
    black pepper

1 For the filling, heat the olive oil in a large frying pan and sauté the onion until tender. Add the crushed garlic and cook for a further 2 minutes. Transfer to a bowl.

2 Remove the skin from the cooked chicken and mince or finely chop the flesh. Add the chicken to the onion with the rest of the filling ingredients. Mix thoroughly and season with salt and pepper. Set aside.

3 Preheat the oven to 190°C/375°F/ Gas 5. Have a damp tea towel ready to keep the filo pastry covered at all times. You will need to work fast, as it dries out quickly when exposed to air. Unravel the pastry and cut the whole batch into a 30 cm/12 in square.

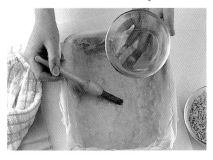

4 Taking half the sheets (cover the remainder), brush one sheet with a little olive oil, lay it on a well-greased 1.35 litre/2¼ pint ovenproof dish and sprinkle with a few chopped toasted almonds. Repeat with the other sheets, overlapping them alternately.

5 Spoon in the filling and cover the pie with the rest of the pastry, overlapping it in the same way.

6 Fold in the overlapping edges and mark a diamond pattern on the surface of the pie with a sharp knife. Brush with milk and sprinkle on any remaining almonds. Bake for 20–30 minutes, or until golden brown.

Chicken Kebabs

Chicken kebabs are easy to prepare and a great favourite. They are ideal for barbecues on hot summer evenings.

Serves 6–8

INGREDIENTS
2 young chickens
1 large onion, grated
2 garlic cloves, crushed
120 ml/4 fl oz/½ cup olive oil
juice of 1 lemon
5 ml/1 tsp paprika
2–3 saffron strands, soaked in 15 ml/1 tbsp
   boiling water
salt and freshly ground black pepper
pitta bread and cos lettuce leaves, to serve

3 Thread the chicken on to long, preferably metal, skewers. If barbecuing, once the coals are ready, cook for 10–15 minutes, turning occasionally. Remember that metal skewers will be hot, therefore handle carefully. Ensure that the chicken is cooked all the way through by inserting the point of a knife to check that the juices are clear.

1 Cut the chicken into small pieces, removing the bone if preferred, and place in a shallow bowl. Mix the grated onion, garlic, olive oil, lemon juice, paprika and saffron, and season with salt and pepper.

2 Pour the marinade over the chicken, turning the chicken so that all the pieces are covered evenly. Cover the bowl loosely with clear film and leave in a cool place to marinate for at least 2 hours.

4 Serve with pitta bread. Or you could remove boneless chicken from the skewers and serve it in pitta bread as a sandwich, accompanied by a garlicky yogurt sauce.

COOK'S TIP: On days when the weather is not as suitable for barbecues as it is in Greece, the kebabs can be cooked under a moderately hot grill for about 10–15 minutes, turning occasionally.

Greek Lamb Sausages with Tomato Sauce

The Greek name for these sausages is *soudzoukakia*. They are delicately flavoured with herbs and spices.

Serves 4

INGREDIENTS
50 g/2 oz/1 cup fresh
   breadcrumbs
150 ml/¼ pint/⅔ cup milk
675 g/1½ lb minced lamb
30 ml/2 tbsp grated onion
3 garlic cloves, crushed
10 ml/2 tsp ground cumin
30 ml/2 tbsp chopped
   fresh parsley
flour, for dusting
olive oil, for frying
600 ml/1 pint/2½ cups passata
5 ml/1 tsp sugar
2 bay leaves
1 small onion, peeled
salt and freshly ground
   black pepper
flat leaf parsley, to garnish

1 In a large bowl, mix together the breadcrumbs and milk. Add the minced lamb, grated onion, garlic, cumin and chopped parsley and season with salt and pepper. Stir to ensure that the lamb is well incorporated.

COOK'S TIP: Passata is sieved tomato and is now widely available from supermarkets in cartons or jars.

2 Shape the mixture with your hands into little fat sausages, about 5 cm/2 in long, and roll them in flour. Heat about 60 ml/4 tbsp olive oil in a frying pan.

3 Fry the sausages, in batches if necessary, for about 8 minutes, turning them carefully until evenly browned and crisp.

4 Put the passata, sugar, bay leaves and whole onion in a pan and simmer for 20 minutes. Add the sausages and cook for 10 minutes more. Serve garnished with parsley.

Lamb Kebabs with Mint

Tender pieces of lamb are marinated in a refreshingly spicy mixture of yogurt, garlic, saffron, mint and honey.

Serves 4

INGREDIENTS

300 ml/½ pint/1¼ cups Greek-style yogurt
½ garlic clove, crushed
pinch of saffron powder
30 ml/2 tbsp chopped fresh mint
30 ml/2 tbsp clear honey
45 ml/3 tbsp olive oil
3 lamb neck fillets, about 675 g/1½ lb
1 medium aubergine
2 small red onions, quartered
salt and freshly ground black pepper
small mint leaves, to garnish
mixed salad and hot pitta bread, to serve

1 In a shallow dish, mix together the yogurt, garlic, saffron, mint, honey, oil and pepper.

2 Trim the lamb and cut into 2.5 cm/1 in cubes. Add to the marinade and stir until well coated. Cover and leave to marinate for at least 4 hours, or preferably overnight.

3 Cut the aubergine into 2.5 cm/1 in cubes and blanch in boiling salted water for 1–2 minutes. Drain well and pat dry on kitchen paper.

4 Remove the lamb cubes from the marinade. Thread the lamb, aubergine and onion pieces alternately on to skewers. Grill for 10–12 minutes, turning and basting occasionally with the marinade, until the lamb is tender.

5 Serve the skewers garnished with mint leaves and accompanied by a mixed salad and hot pitta bread.

COOK'S TIP: If you are using bamboo skewers, soak them in cold water before use to prevent them from burning.

Moussaka

Kefalotiri, a hard cheese made with sheep's or goat's milk, makes the perfect topping for a classic moussaka.

Serves 6

INGREDIENTS
2 large aubergines, thinly sliced
45 ml/3 tbsp olive oil
675 g/1½ lb lean minced beef
1 onion, chopped
2 garlic cloves, crushed
2 large fresh tomatoes,
   chopped
120 ml/4 fl oz/½ cup dry white wine
45 ml/3 tbsp chopped fresh parsley
45 ml/3 tbsp fresh breadcrumbs
2 egg whites
salt and freshly ground black pepper

FOR THE TOPPING
40 g/1½ oz/3 tbsp butter
40 g/1½ oz/⅓ cup plain flour
400 ml/14 fl oz/1⅔ cups milk
2.5 ml/½ tsp freshly grated nutmeg
150 g/5 oz/1¼ cups grated Kefalotiri
   or hard sheep's or goat's cheese
2 egg yolks, plus 1 whole egg

1 Layer the sliced aubergines in a colander, sprinkling each layer with salt. Allow to drain for 20 minutes, then rinse and pat dry with kitchen paper. Preheat the oven to 190°C/ 375°F/Gas 5. Spread out the aubergines in a roasting tin, brush with olive oil, then bake for 10 minutes, until just softened. Remove and set aside to cool.

2 Heat the remaining oil in a large saucepan and brown the minced beef, stirring frequently, until crumbly. Add the onion and garlic and cook for a further 5 minutes.

3 Add the tomatoes and stir in the wine. Season with salt and pepper to taste. Bring to the boil, lower the heat, cover and simmer for 15 minutes. Remove from the heat, leave to cool for about 10 minutes, then stir in the parsley, breadcrumbs and egg whites.

4 Lightly grease a large ovenproof dish, then spread half the aubergines on the base. Spread over the sauce, then top with the remaining aubergines.

5 To make the topping, put the butter, flour and milk in a saucepan. Bring to the boil over a low heat, whisking until the mixture thickens to form a smooth, creamy sauce. Lower the heat and simmer for 2 minutes. Remove from the heat, season and stir in the nutmeg and half the cheese.

6 Allow to cool for 5 minutes, then beat in the egg yolks and the whole egg. Pour the sauce over the top layer of aubergines and sprinkle with the remaining kefalotiri cheese. Bake the moussaka for 30–40 minutes, or until the topping is golden brown. Allow the dish to stand for 10 minutes before serving.

Pastitsio

Another excellent main meal, this recipe is both economical and filling, as well as being easy to prepare.

Serves 4

INGREDIENTS
15 ml/1 tbsp oil
450 g/1 lb/4 cups minced lamb
1 onion, chopped
2 garlic cloves, crushed
30 ml/2 tbsp tomato purée
25 g/1 oz/2 tbsp plain flour
300 ml/½ pint/1¼ cups lamb stock
2 large tomatoes
115 g/4 oz/1 cup pasta shapes
450 g/1 lb Greek-style yogurt
2 eggs
salt and freshly ground black pepper
crisp salad, to serve

3 Stir in the stock and season to taste. Bring to the boil and cook for 20 minutes.

4 Slice the tomatoes, place the meat in an ovenproof dish and arrange the tomatoes on top.

1 Preheat the oven to 190°C/375°F/ Gas 5. Heat the oil and fry the lamb for 5 minutes. Add the onion and garlic and fry for a further 5 minutes.

2 Stir the tomato purée and flour into the lamb mixture. Continue to cook for 1 minute.

5 Cook the pasta shapes in a saucepan of boiling salted water for 8–10 minutes, or until tender, but still firm to the bite. Drain well.

6 Mix together the pasta, yogurt and eggs. Spoon on top of the tomatoes and cook in the oven for 1 hour. Serve with a crisp salad.

Kleftiko

For this recipe, marinated lamb steaks or chops are slow-cooked to develop an unbeatable, meltingly tender flavour.

Serves 4

INGREDIENTS
juice of 1 lemon
15 ml/1 tbsp chopped fresh oregano
4 lamb leg steaks or chump chops with
    bones
30 ml/2 tbsp olive oil
2 large onions, thinly sliced
2 bay leaves
150 ml/¼ pint/⅔ cup dry white wine
225 g/8 oz/2 cups plain flour
salt and freshly ground black pepper
boiled potatoes, to serve

1 Mix together the lemon juice, oregano and salt and pepper, and brush over both sides of the lamb. Leave to marinate for at least 4 hours.

2 Preheat the oven to 160°C/325°F/ Gas 3. Drain the lamb, reserving the marinade, and dry with kitchen paper. Heat the oil in a large frying pan and fry the lamb over a high heat until browned on both sides.

3 Transfer the lamb to a shallow pie dish and arrange evenly over the bottom. Scatter the sliced onions and bay leaves around it, then pour over the wine and reserved marinade.

4 Mix the flour with sufficient cold water to make a firm dough. Moisten the rim of the pie dish with water. Roll out the dough on a floured surface and use to cover the dish so that it is tightly sealed, enclosing the lamb completely.

5 Bake for 2 hours, then break away the dough crust and serve the lamb hot with boiled potatoes.

COOK'S TIP: Lamb steaks or chops with bones are not absolutely essential for this recipe, but the bones will provide the dish with lots of additional flavour.

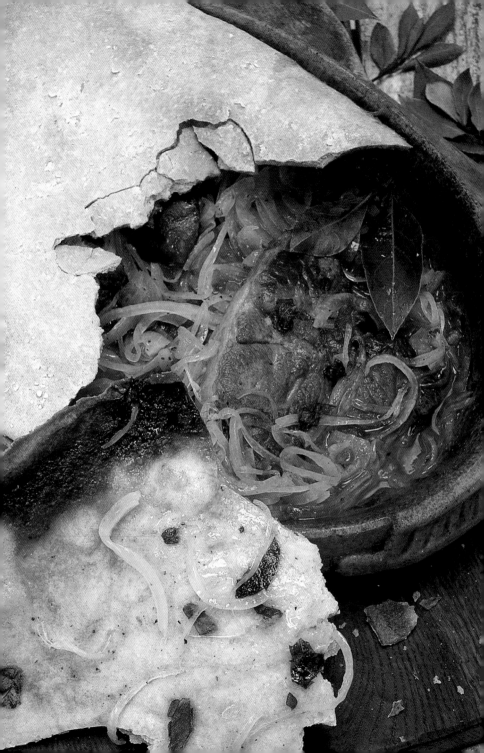

Spanakopitta

There are several ways of making this popular spinach and filo pastry pie, but feta cheese is always included.

Serves 6

INGREDIENTS
1 kg/2¼ lb fresh spinach
4 spring onions, chopped
300 g/11 oz feta cheese, crumbled
2 large eggs, beaten
30 ml/2 tbsp chopped fresh parsley
15 ml/1 tbsp chopped fresh dill
45 ml/3 tbsp currants (optional)
about 8 filo pastry sheets, each about
    30 x 18 cm/12 x 7 in
150 ml/¼ pint/⅔ cup olive oil
freshly ground black pepper

2 Place the spinach in a bowl with the spring onions and cheese, then pour in the eggs. Mix in the herbs and currants (if using). Season with pepper.

3 Brush a filo sheet with oil and fit it into a 23 cm/9 in pie dish, allowing it to hang over the edges. Top with 3–4 more sheets at different angles, brushing each one with oil.

4 Spoon in the filling, then top with all but one of the remaining filo sheets, brushing each with oil. Fold in the overhanging filo. Brush the reserved filo with oil and scrunch it over the top of the pie.

1 Preheat the oven to 190°C/375°F/ Gas 5. Break off any thick stalks from the spinach, then blanch the leaves in a very small amount of boiling water for 1–2 minutes, until just wilted. Drain and refresh under cold water. Drain again, squeeze dry and chop roughly.

5 Brush the pie with oil. Sprinkle with a little water to stop the filo edges from curling, then place on a baking sheet. Bake for about 40 minutes, until golden and crisp. Cool the pie for 15 minutes before serving.

Peppers with Rice, Feta & Pine Nut Stuffing

A popular, filling and nutritious family supper dish, which can be prepared ahead and reheated as required.

Serves 4

INGREDIENTS
4 large red, green or yellow peppers, or a mixture
475 ml/16 fl oz/2 cups vegetable stock
200 g/7 oz/1 cup long grain rice
30 ml/2 tbsp olive oil
1 onion, chopped
2 garlic cloves, crushed
115 g/4 oz/1½ cups button mushrooms, chopped
1 carrot, grated
4 tomatoes, chopped
15 ml/1 tbsp chopped fresh dill
90 g/3½ oz feta cheese, crumbled
75 g/3 oz/¾ cup pine nuts, lightly toasted
30 ml/2 tbsp currants
25 g/1 oz/⅓ cup freshly grated Parmesan cheese
salt and freshly ground black pepper
salad of mixed leaves, to serve

1 Preheat the oven to 190°C/375°F/ Gas 5. Cut the peppers in half lengthways and remove the cores and seeds. Bring a large saucepan of water to the boil, add the peppers and blanch for 5 minutes. Remove from the pan, drain upside-down, then place, hollow up, in a lightly greased baking dish.

2 Put the stock in another saucepan. Add the rice, bring to the boil, then lower the heat. Cover and simmer gently for 15 minutes. Remove the pan from the heat without lifting the lid and leave to stand in a warm place for 5 minutes.

3 Meanwhile, heat the olive oil and sauté the onion and garlic for 5 minutes. Stir in the mushrooms, carrot and tomatoes with salt and pepper to taste. Cover, cook for 5 minutes, until softened, then mix in the rice, dill, feta, pine nuts and currants.

4 Divide the mixture among the pepper halves, sprinkle over the Parmesan and bake for 20 minutes, or until the topping has browned. Serve with a mixed salad.

Pilaff with Saffron & Pickled Walnuts

Pickled walnuts have a warm, tangy flavour that is lovely in rice dishes. This pilaff is interesting enough to serve on its own.

Serves 4

INGREDIENTS
5 ml/1 tsp saffron strands
40 g/1½ oz/½ cup pine nuts
45 ml/3 tbsp olive oil
1 large onion, chopped
3 garlic cloves, crushed
1.5 ml/¼ tsp ground allspice
4 cm/1½ in piece fresh root ginger, grated
225 g/8 oz/generous 1 cup long grain rice
300 ml/½ pint/1¼ cups vegetable stock
50 g/2 oz/½ cup pickled walnuts, drained and roughly chopped
40 g/1½ oz/¼ cup raisins
45 ml/3 tbsp roughly chopped parsley or fresh coriander
salt and freshly ground black pepper
parsley or coriander, to garnish
Greek-style yogurt, to serve

1 Put the saffron in a bowl with 15 ml/1 tbsp boiling water and leave to stand. Heat a large frying pan and dry fry the pine nuts until they turn golden. Set them aside.

2 Heat the oil in the pan and fry the onion, garlic and allspice for 3 minutes. Stir in the ginger and rice and cook for 1 minute.

3 Add the stock and bring to the boil. Reduce the heat, cover and simmer gently for 15 minutes, until the rice is just tender.

4 Stir in the saffron and liquid, along with the fried pine nuts, pickled walnuts, raisins and chopped parsley or coriander. Season to taste with salt and freshly ground black pepper. Heat the pilaff through gently for 2 minutes. Garnish with parsley or coriander leaves and serve with Greek-style yogurt.

COOK'S TIP: Use one small aubergine, chopped and fried in a little olive oil, instead of the pickled walnuts, if you prefer.

Spiced Turnips with Spinach & Tomatoes

Sweet baby turnips, tender spinach and ripe tomatoes make tempting partners in this simple vegetable stew.

Serves 6

INGREDIENTS

450 g/1 lb plum or other well-
    flavoured tomatoes
60 ml/4 tbsp olive oil
2 onions, sliced
450 g/1 lb baby turnips, peeled
5 ml/1 tsp paprika
2.5 ml/½ tsp caster sugar
60 ml/4 tbsp chopped fresh coriander
450 g/1 lb fresh young spinach,
    stalks removed
salt and freshly ground
    black pepper

1 Make a small nick in the skins of the tomatoes and plunge them into a bowl of boiling water for 30 seconds, then refresh them in a bowl of cold water. Peel away the tomato skins and chop the flesh roughly. Set aside. Heat the olive oil in a large frying pan and fry the onion slices for about 5 minutes, until golden.

COOK'S TIP: In Greece, cooks do not like to waste the tops of root vegetables. Like radish and beetroot tops, turnip tops are delicious boiled and served cold with a simple dressing of lemon juice and olive oil.

2 Add the peeled baby turnips, chopped tomatoes and paprika to the pan with 60 ml/4 tbsp water and cook until the tomatoes have become pulpy. Cover the pan and continue cooking until the baby turnips have softened.

3 Stir in the caster sugar and chopped coriander, then add the prepared spinach and a little salt and freshly ground black pepper and cook for a further 2–3 minutes, until the spinach has wilted. Serve the stew warm or cold.

Classic Greek Salad

If you have ever visited Greece you will know that a Greek salad with a chunk of bread makes a delicious, filling meal.

Serves 4

INGREDIENTS
1 cos lettuce
½ cucumber, halved lengthways and sliced
4 tomatoes, cut into wedges
8 spring onions
75 g/3 oz/2½ cups Greek black olives
115 g/4 oz feta cheese
90 ml/6 tbsp white wine vinegar
150 ml/¼ pint/⅔ cup extra virgin
   olive oil
salt and freshly ground black pepper
extra olives and fresh bread, to serve
   (optional)

1 Tear the lettuce leaves into pieces and place them in a large mixing bowl. Add the sliced cucumber and wedges of tomato.

2 Slice the spring onions. Add with the olives and toss well. Add cubes of feta cheese. Whisk together the vinegar, oil and seasoning, pour over the salad and toss well.

COOK'S TIP: Assemble in advance and chill, without dressing. Keep the dressing at room temperature.

Tomato & Feta Cheese Salad

Sweet sun-ripened tomatoes are rarely more delicious than when served with feta cheese and olive oil.

Serves 4

INGREDIENTS
900 g/2 lb tomatoes
200 g/7 oz feta cheese
120 ml/4 fl oz/½ cup olive oil
12 black olives
4 sprigs fresh basil
freshly ground black pepper

1 Remove the tough cores from the tomatoes with a small, sharp knife. Slice them thickly and arrange in a shallow dish, overlapping the slices slightly.

2 Crumble the feta cheese over the slices of tomato, sprinkle with olive oil, then strew with black olives and fresh basil. Season with freshly ground black pepper and serve at room temperature. The salad can be enjoyed as a light meal in itself, accompanied by plenty of crispy bread.

COOK'S TIP: Feta cheese has a strong flavour and can be salty. The least salty variety is imported from Greece and is available from specialist delicatessens.

Warm Broad Bean & Feta Salad

Serve as a starter or accompaniment.

Serves 4–6

INGREDIENTS
900 g/2 lb broad beans, shelled
60 ml/4 tbsp olive oil
175 g/6 oz plum tomatoes, halved, or
    quartered, if large
4 garlic cloves, crushed
115 g/4 oz firm feta cheese,
    cut into chunks
45 ml/3 tbsp chopped fresh dill
12 black olives
salt and freshly ground black pepper
chopped fresh dill,
    to garnish

1 Cook the broad beans in a pan of boiling, salted water until just tender. Drain and set aside.

2 Meanwhile, heat the oil in a heavy-based frying pan and add the tomatoes and garlic. Cook, stirring, until the tomatoes are beginning to change colour.

3 Add the feta cheese to the pan and toss the ingredients together for 1 minute. Mix with the cooked beans, chopped dill, black olives and salt and pepper. Serve garnished with extra chopped dill.

Halloumi & Grape Salad

Sweet and savoury – a perfect match!

Serves 4

INGREDIENTS
150 g/5 oz mixed green salad leaves
75 g/3 oz seedless green grapes
75 g/3 oz seedless black grapes
250 g/9 oz halloumi cheese
45 ml/3 tbsp olive oil
fresh young thyme leaves or dill,
    to garnish

FOR THE DRESSING
60 ml/4 tbsp olive oil
15 ml/1 tbsp lemon juice
2.5 ml/½ tsp caster sugar
salt and freshly ground black pepper
15 ml/1 tbsp chopped fresh thyme or dill

1 Make the dressing. Combine the oil, lemon juice and sugar with a whisk or fork. Season. Stir in the thyme or dill and set aside.

2 Toss together the salad leaves and grapes, then transfer to a large serving plate. Thinly slice the cheese. Heat the oil in a large frying pan. Add the cheese and fry until golden on the underside. Turn and cook the other side. Arrange over the salad. Pour over the dressing and garnish with thyme or dill.

Baklava

This sweet and spicy pie is made from layers of buttered filo pastry packed with nuts and sweetened with a honey and lemon syrup.

Makes 10 pieces

INGREDIENTS
6 large sheets of filo pastry
75 g/3 oz/6 tbsp butter, melted
225 g/8 oz/2 cups chopped mixed nuts
   (such as almonds, pistachios,
   hazelnuts and walnuts)
50 g/2 oz/1 cup fresh
   breadcrumbs
5 ml/1 tsp ground cinnamon
5 ml/1 tsp mixed spice
2.5 ml/½ tsp grated nutmeg
250 ml/8 fl oz/1 cup clear honey
60 ml/4 tbsp lemon juice

1 Preheat the oven to 180°C/350°F/
Gas 4. Butter an 18 x 28 cm/
7 x 11 in tin. Unroll the pastry, brush
one sheet with melted butter (keep the
remainder covered with a slightly
damp tea towel while you work) and
use to line the tin, easing it carefully
up the sides.

2 Brush two more sheets with butter
and lay on top of the base sheet,
easing the pastry into the corners and
letting the edges overhang.

3 Mix together the nuts, breadcrumbs
and spices in a bowl and spoon this
mixture into the lined tin.

4 Cut the remaining three sheets of
pastry in half widthways and brush
each one with a little of the butter.
Layer the sheets on top of the filling
and fold in any overhanging edges.
Cut the baklava diagonally into
diamonds. Bake in the oven for about
30 minutes, until golden.

5 Meanwhile, heat the honey and
lemon juice together in a pan.
When the baklava is cooked, remove
from the oven and pour the syrup
over while the baklava is still warm.
Leave to cool completely, re-cut into
diamonds and serve.

Fresh Figs with Honey & Wine

Any variety of figs can be used in this recipe, their ripeness determining the cooking time. Choose ones that are plump and firm.

Serves 6

INGREDIENTS
450 ml/¾ pint/scant 2 cups dry
    white wine
75 g/3 oz/⅓ cup clear honey
50 g/2 oz/¼ cup caster sugar
1 small orange
8 whole cloves
450 g/1 lb fresh figs
1 cinnamon stick
  bay leaves, to decorate

FOR THE CREAM
300 ml/½ pint/1¼ cups
    double cream
1 vanilla pod
5 ml/1 tsp caster sugar

1 Put the wine, honey and sugar in a heavy-based saucepan and heat gently until the sugar dissolves.

2 Stud the orange with the cloves and add to the syrup with the figs and cinnamon. Simmer very gently for 5–10 minutes, until the figs are softened. Transfer to a serving dish and leave to cool. Decorate with bay leaves.

3 Put 150 ml/¼ pint/⅔ cup of the cream in a pan with the vanilla. Bring almost to the boil, then leave to cool and infuse for 30 minutes. Remove the vanilla. Whip with the remaining cream and sugar. Transfer to a serving dish and serve with the figs.

Fruit with Honey Dip

For an authentic touch, use Hymettus honey. It is expensive, but is deliciously aromatic and tastes of thyme.

Serves 4

INGREDIENTS
225 g/8 oz/1 cup
    Greek-style yogurt
45 ml/3 tbsp clear honey
selection of fresh fruit for dipping, such as
    apples, pears, figs, tangerines, grapes,
    cherries, strawberries and kiwi fruit

1 Place the Greek-style yogurt in a mixing bowl, beat until smooth, then stir in the honey, leaving a little marbled effect.

2 Use a sharp knife to cut the fruits into wedges or bite-size pieces, or leave whole.

3 Arrange the fruits attractively on a platter with the bowl of honey dip in the centre. Serve chilled.

COOK'S TIP: Avoid sticky fingers by providing individual finger bowls of warm water.

Greek Honey & Lemon Cake

This delicately flavoured, light sponge cake makes a delicious treat with a cup of strong, Greek coffee.

Makes 16 slices

INGREDIENTS
40 g/1½ oz/3 tbsp sunflower margarine
60 ml/4 tbsp clear honey
finely grated rind and juice of 1 lemon
150 ml/¼ pint/⅔ cup milk
150 g/5 oz/1¼ cups plain flour
7.5 ml/1½ tsp baking powder
2.5 ml/½ tsp grated nutmeg
50 g/2 oz/¼ cup semolina
2 egg whites
10 ml/2 tsp sesame seeds

1 Preheat the oven to 200°C/400°F/ Gas 6. Lightly oil a 19 cm/7½ in square deep cake tin and line the base with non-stick baking paper.

3 In a mixing bowl, sift together the flour, baking powder and nutmeg, then beat into the milk mixture with the semolina. Whisk the egg whites until they form soft peaks, then fold evenly into the mixture.

2 Place the margarine and 45 ml/ 3 tbsp of the honey in a saucepan and heat gently until melted. Reserve 15 ml/1 tbsp lemon juice, then stir in the rest with the lemon rind and milk.

4 Spoon into the tin and sprinkle with sesame seeds. Bake for 25–30 minutes, until golden brown on top. Mix the reserved honey and lemon juice and drizzle over the cake while warm. Cool in the tin, then cut into fingers to serve.

Olive & Oregano Bread

This is an excellent accompaniment to all salads and is particularly good served warm.

Serves 8–10

INGREDIENTS
300 ml/½ pint/1¼ cups warm water
5 ml/1 tsp dried yeast
pinch of sugar
15 ml/1 tbsp olive oil
1 onion, chopped
450 g/1 lb/4 cups strong white flour
5 ml/1 tsp salt
1.5 ml/¼ tsp freshly ground black pepper
50 g/2 oz/⅓ cup stoned black olives,
　roughly chopped
15 ml/1 tbsp black olive paste
15 ml/1 tbsp chopped fresh oregano
15 ml/1 tbsp chopped fresh parsley

1 Put half the warm water in a jug. Sprinkle the dried yeast on top. Add the sugar, mix well and leave for 10 minutes.

2 Heat the olive oil in a frying pan and fry the chopped onion until golden brown.

3 Sift the flour into a large mixing bowl with the salt and pepper. Make a well in the centre. Add the dried yeast mixture, the fried onion (with the oil), the olives, olive paste, oregano, parsley and remaining water. Gradually incorporate the flour and mix to a soft dough, adding a little extra water if necessary.

4 Turn the dough on to a floured surface and knead for 5 minutes, until smooth and elastic. Place in a mixing bowl, cover with a damp tea towel and leave in a warm place to rise for about 2 hours, until doubled in bulk. Lightly grease a baking sheet.

5 Turn the dough on to a floured surface and knead again for a few minutes. Shape into a 20 cm/8 in round and place on the prepared baking sheet. Using a sharp knife, make criss-cross cuts over the top, cover and leave in a warm place for 30 minutes, until well risen. Preheat the oven to 220°C/425°F/Gas 7.

6 Dust the loaf with a little flour. Bake for 10 minutes, then lower the oven temperature to 200°C/ 400°F/Gas 6. Continue to bake for 20 minutes more, or until the loaf sounds hollow when it is tapped underneath. Transfer to a wire rack to cool slightly before serving.

Greek Easter Bread

In Greece, Easter celebrations are very important. This bread is sold in all the bakers' shops, and also made at home. It is traditionally decorated with red dyed eggs.

Makes 1 loaf

INGREDIENTS
25 g/1 oz fresh yeast
120 ml/4 fl oz/½ cup warm milk
675 g/1½ lb/6 cups strong
    plain flour
2 eggs, beaten
2.5 ml/½ tsp caraway seeds
15 ml/1 tbsp caster sugar
15 ml/1 tbsp brandy
50 g/2 oz/4 tbsp butter, melted
1 egg white, beaten
2–3 hard-boiled eggs, dyed red
    with cochineal food colouring
50 g/2 oz/½ cup split almonds

1 Crumble the yeast into a bowl. Mix with 15–30 ml/1–2 tbsp warm water, until softened. Add the milk and 115 g/4 oz/1 cup of the flour and mix to a creamy consistency. Cover with a cloth, and leave in a warm place to rise for 1 hour or until it is about double its original size.

2 Sift the remaining flour into a large bowl and make a well in the centre. Pour the risen yeast into the well and draw in a little of the flour from the sides. Add the eggs, caraway seeds, sugar and brandy. Incorporate the remaining flour, until the mixture begins to form a dough.

3 Mix in the melted butter. Turn on to a floured surface and knead for about 10 minutes, until the dough becomes smooth. Return to the bowl and cover with a cloth. Leave in a warm place for 3 hours.

4 Preheat the oven to 180°C/350°F/ Gas 4. Knock back the dough, turn on to a floured surface and knead for a minute or two. Divide the dough into three and roll each piece into a long sausage. Make a plait as shown and place the loaf on a greased baking sheet.

5 Tuck the ends under, brush with the egg white and decorate with the eggs and split almonds. Bake for about 1 hour, until the loaf sounds hollow when tapped on the bottom. Cool on a wire rack.

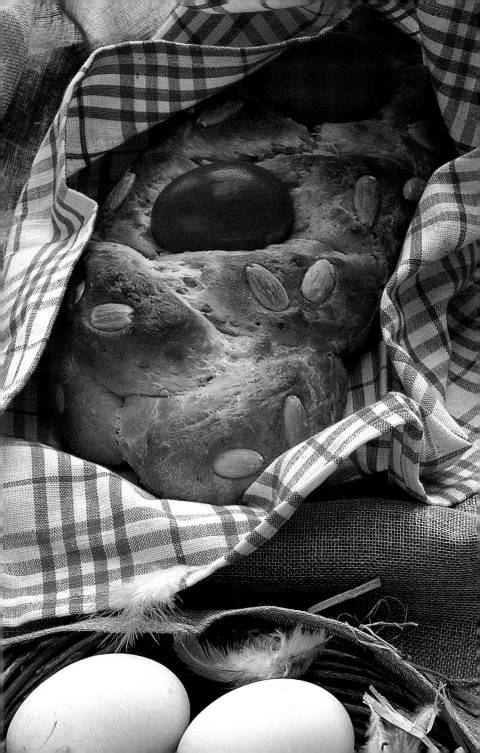

Index

First published in 1999 by Lorenz Books © Anness Publishing Limited 1999

Lorenz Books is an imprint of Anness Publishing Limited, Hermes House, 88-89 Blackfriars Road, London SE1 8HA

This edition distributed in Canada by Raincoast Books, 8680 Cambie Street, Vancouver, British Columbia V6P 6M9

ISBN 0 7548 0144 6

A CIP catalogue record for this book is available from the British Library.

Publisher: Joanna Lorenz
Editor: Valerie Ferguson
Series Designer: Bobbie Colgate Stone
Designer: Andrew Heath
Editorial Reader: Marion Wilson
Production Controller: Joanna King

Recipes contributed by: Roz Denny, Matthew Drennan, Joanna Farrow, Christine France, Sarah Gates, Shirley Gill, Carole Handslip, Soheila Kimberley, Sue Maggs, Jenny Stacey, Liz Trigg, Steven Wheeler

Photography: William Adams-Lingwood, Karl Adamson, Edward Allwright, Steve Baxter, James Duncan, Michelle Garrett, John Heseltine, Amanda Heywood, Ferguson Hill, Patrick McLeavey

1 3 5 7 9 10 8 6 4 2

Notes:
For all recipes, quantities are given in both metric and imperial measures and, where appropriate, measures are also given in standard cups and spoons. Follow one set, but not a mixture, because they are not interchangeable.
Standard spoon and cup measures are level.
1 tsp = 5 ml 1 tbsp = 15 ml
1 cup = 250 ml/8 fl oz

Australian standard tablespoons are 20 ml. Australian readers should use 3 tsp in place of 1 tbsp for measuring small quantities of gelatine, cornflour, salt, etc.

Medium eggs are used unless otherwise stated.

Printed in Singapore